Bible Interpretations

Eleventh Series

January 7 - March 25, 1894

Genesis, Proverbs, Mark

Bible
Interpretations

Eleventh Series

Genesis, Proverbs, Mark

These Bible Interpretations were published in the
Inter-Ocean Newspaper in Chicago, Illinois during the
late eighteen nineties.

By

Emma Curtis Hopkins

*President of the Emma Curtis Hopkins Theological
Seminary in Chicago, Illinois*

WISEWOMAN PRESS

Bible Interpretations: Eleventh Series

By Emma Curtis Hopkins

© WiseWoman Press 2011

Managing Editor: Michael Terranova

ISBN: 978-0945385-61-5

WiseWoman Press

Vancouver, WA 98665

www.wisewomanpress.com

www.emmacurtishopkins.com

CONTENTS

Editors Note

All lessons starting with the Seventh Series of Bible Interpretations will be Sunday postings from the Inter-Ocean Newspaper in Chicago, Illinois. Many of the lessons in the following series were retrieved from the International New Thought Association Archives, in Mesa, Arizona by, Rev Joanna Rogers. Many others were retrieved from libraries in Chicago, and the Library of Congress, by Rev. Natalie Jean.

All the lessons follow the Sunday School Lesson Plan published in "Peloubet's International Sunday School Lessons". The passages to be studied are selected by an International Committee of traditional Bible Scholars.

Some of the Emma's lessons don't have a title. In these cases the heading will say "Comments and Explanations of the Golden Text," followed by the Bible passages to be studied.

Foreword

By Rev. Natalie R. Jean

I have read many teachings by Emma Curtis Hopkins, but the teachings that touch the very essence of my soul are her Bible Interpretations. There are many books written on the teachings of the Bible, but none can touch the surface of the true messages more than these Bible interpretations. With each word you can feel and see how Spirit spoke through Emma. The mystical interpretations take you on a wonderful journey to Self Realization.

Each passage opens your consciousness to a new awareness of the realities of life. The illusions of life seem to disappear through each interpretation. Emma teaches that we are the key that unlocks the doorway to the light that shines within. She incorporates ideals of other religions into her teachings, in order to understand the commonalities, so that there is a complete understanding of our Oneness. Emma opens our eyes and mind to a better today and exciting future.

Emma Curtis Hopkins, one of the Founders of New Thought teaches us to love ourselves, to speak our Truth, and to focus on our Good. My life has moved in wonderful directions because of her teachings. I know the only thing that can move me in this world is God. May these interpretations guide you to a similar path and may you truly remember that "There Is Good For You and You Ought to Have It."

Introduction

Emma Curtis Hopkins was born in 1849 in Killingsly, Connecticut. She passed on April 8, 1925. Mrs. Hopkins had a marvelous education and could read many of the worlds classical texts in their original language. During her extensive studies she was always able to discover the Universal Truths in each of the world's sacred traditions. She quotes from many of these teachings in her writings. As she was a very private person, we know little about her personal life. What we do know has been gleaned from other people or from the archived writings we have been able to discover.

Emma Curtis Hopkins was one of the greatest influences on the New Thought movement in the United States. She taught over 50,000 people the Universal Truth of knowing "God is All there is." She taught many of founders of early New Thought, and in turn these individuals expanded the influence of her teachings. All of her writings encourage the student to enter into a personal relationship with God. She presses us to deny anything except the Truth of this spiritual Presence in every area of our lives. This is the central focus of all her teachings.

The first six series of Bible Interpretations were presented at her seminary in Chicago, Illinois. The remaining Series', probably close to thirty, were printed in the Inter Ocean Newspaper in Chicago. Many of the lessons are no longer available for various reasons. It is the intention of WiseWoman Press to publish as many of these Bible Interpretations as possible. Our hope is that any missing lessons will be found or directed to us.

I am very honored to join the long line of people that have been involved in publishing Emma Curtis Hopkins's Bible Interpretations. Some confusion exists as to the numbering sequence of the lessons. In the early 1920's many of the lessons were published by the Highwatch Fellowship. Inadvertently the first two lessons were omitted from the numbering system. Rev. Joanna Rogers has corrected this mistake by finding the first two lessons and restoring them to their rightful place in the order. Rev. Rogers has been able to find many of the missing lessons at the International New Thought Alliance archives in Mesa, Arizona. Rev. Rogers painstakingly scoured the archives for the missing lessons as well as for Mrs. Hopkins other works. She has published much of what was discovered. WiseWoman Press is now publishing the correctly numbered series of the Bible Interpretations.

In the early 1940's, there was a resurgence of interest in Emma's works. At that time, Highwatch Fellowship began to publish many of her writings, and it was then that *High Mysticism*, her seminal work was published. Previously, the material contained in High Mysticism was only available as individual lessons and was brought together in book form for the first time. Although there were many errors in these first publications and many Bible verses were incorrectly quoted, I am happy to announce that WiseWoman Press is now publishing *High Mysticism* in the a corrected format. This corrected form was scanned faithfully from the original, individual lessons.

The next person to publish some of the Bible Lessons was Rev. Marge Flotron from the Ministry of Truth International in Chicago, Illinois. She published the Bible Lessons as well as many of Emma's other works. By her initiative, Emma's writings were brought to a larger audience when DeVorss & Company, a longtime publisher of Truth Teachings, took on the publication of her key works.

In addition, Dr. Carmelita Trowbridge, founding minister of The Sanctuary of Truth in Alhambra, California, inspired her assistant minister, Rev. Shirley Lawrence, to publish many of Emma's works, including the first three series of Bible Interpretations. Rev. Lawrence created mail order courses for many of these Series. She has graciously passed on any information she had, in order to assure that these works continue to inspire individuals and groups who are called to further study of the teachings of Mrs. Hopkins.

Finally, a very special acknowledgement goes to Rev Natalie Jean, who has worked diligently to retrieve several of Emma's lessons from the Library of Congress, as well as libraries in Chicago. Rev. Jean hand-typed many of the lessons she found on microfilm. Much of what she found is on her website, www.highwatch.net.

It is with a grateful heart that I am able to pass on these wonderful teachings. I have been studying dear Emma's works for fifteen years. I was introduced to her writings by my mentor and teacher, Rev. Marcia Sutton. I have been overjoyed with the results of delving deeply into these Truth Teachings.

In 2004, I wrote a Sacred Covenant entitled "Resurrecting Emma," and created a website, www.emmacurtishopkins.com. The result of creating this covenant and website has brought many of Emma's works into my hands and has deepened my faith in God. As a result of my love for these works, I was led to become a member of Wise-Woman Press and to publish these wonderful teachings. God is Good.

My understanding of Truth from these divinely inspired teachings keeps bringing great Joy, Freedom, and Peace to my life.

Dear reader; It is with an open heart that I offer these works to you, and I know they will touch you as they have touched me. Together we are living in the Truth that God is truly present, and living for and through each of us.

The greatest Truth Emma presented to us is "My Good is my God, Omnipresent, Omnipotent and Omniscient."

Rev. Michael Terranova

WiseWoman Press

Vancouver, Washington, 2010

LESSON I

The First Adam

Genesis 1:26-31 Genesis 2:1-3

With today's lesson we begin a six years' course of scripture study. The purpose of the committee on lessons is to take us on a journey through the history of man from his fall to his redemption as related in the Christian Hebrew Bible.

We start out with Genesis first and second chapters. The first chapter tells of spiritual man. The second tells of material appearance. The third chapter admits that all things upon the earth were created invisibly before they exposed themselves physically. The second chapter shows itself to be the description of the symbolic and unreal because it presents man upside down from his first estate. As trees reflected in water show top downward so the lofty godliness of man and earth as first pronounced "good" by the almighty truth is pictured "fallen" when explained secondly from the physical-sense standpoint.

1

The physical senses are the obedient servants of the language of man. They are the folded leaves of a book. They are able to unroll and extend to the infinite stretches of observation of all things in creation. They show forth now as matter in all its forms. When we tell them to proceed further and see beyond what they now do we shall see further, and the sounds of the mornings on Polaris will be easy to hear.

There is a man now in Chicago, who has talked to his muscles till he has trained them to lift nearly a ton's weight. One muscle only remains obdurate, not yet yielding to his talking. When that succumbs he will lift the ton. Then who shall say that those muscles which are willing to respond so far may not respond farther? Who shall limit the strength of the man described in Genesis first? May he not come forth clearer and clearer as right language is used?

Language is Jehovah God. It is written, "The word was God." The first man spiritual can see all things. There is nothing can obstruct his views. He is "good" in every faculty. He can hear and touch everything. Within us is that "good" man with all his good facilities and good possessions. As it is written *"Christ in you."* (Colossians 1:27)

Man the Image of Language.

The man who has trained his muscles by talking to them shows the dominion language. Man is in the image and likeness of the language used to formulate him. It was once sacrilegious to think of the "six days" of creation as referring to periods of time. It expanded the thoughts of men when they alluded to vast extents of time and at once men were younger in feeling. It made all men younger at 60 than they had formerly been considered at 40. In Hamlet's address to his mother we would think she must be an aged fright, while from the customs of those times she must not be much past 30. Contemplation of vast and unnamed spaces of activities as forever unrolling has extended the youth of mankind. Who shall say that purer and truer contemplation may not expose the eternal youth of the "Elohim" — sons of God — ourselves? The language of truth is contemplation. "Have dominion over every living thing," says the God in man to all mankind. This lesson is a trumpet-call to notice how pure talking is the actual arising from beds of limitation to set forth into the open tells of freedom.

It is written. "Arise, let us go hence." On the strength of our pure and unafraid language we will arise from hindrances and go unhindered into the light.

There is one name of pure speech that is not much used. It is light. The city had no need of the sun, for God was its light. God is language. "Thy sun shall no more go down" when thy language never descends. Ruskin tells us that the sun is the power of man's arms and the sun is the power of his mind. Hear this: "Today, in the strength of your youth, you may know what it is to have the power of the sun taken out of your legs and arms. But when you are old, you will know what it is to have the power of the sun taken out of your mind also. Such a thing may happen to you sometimes, even now, but it will continually happen to you, when you are my age. You will no more, then, think over a matter to any good purpose after 12 o'clock in the day. *Sol illuminatis nostra est; Sol salus nostra;Sol sapientia nostr^* — Eagle's Nest, p.365.

Paul and Elymas

The sun of mind is Truth. The darkness of mind is the talk that hides truth. Paul struck Elymas blind by his condemnation of him for not being more and knowing more. Elymas represents money. Money represents obedience of things to thoughts. "I would be more and show you many places and give you many opportunities gladly," said Elymas. "You know nothing and you amount to almost nothing," said Paul. So Elymas groped in darkness. To your money you say, "You know nothing, and are altogether too little to show me the world to get me what I want." So your obedient money gropes around showing you none of its possibilities except as what you wish it might be. Why is this when you have dominion over the earth? Shall you not now seize upon your majesty and talk more -wisely to your Elymas?

The lame man at the beautiful gate represents mankind sitting in obstacle. "Peter and John in the firm and gracious words of Jehovah, "have dominion over every creeping thing." Our hopes and faith are able to dissolve every hindrance. They can fly on free wings of prosperity.

"We shall not fade nor fall,

While faith and hope prevail.

Think this moment of the most beautiful object your eyes ever beheld. Remember it for a brief space of time. Has not your mind sat at this gate looking at your poverty, or at your debt, or at your disease long enough so that you are willing to remember for a time the most beautiful object you ever beheld? Now let these two faces gaze into yours. First, "You are free." Second "Your own words are capable of making you equal with God himself." Look at them with the memory of that beautiful object in your mind. A miracle will be wrought on the line you are not expecting one. The lame man asked for gold and got strong feet. The prayer you have been praying is not answered by looking up to the sun-tipped cherubs on the gate at whose base your hindered feet ache. But something you have not asked to happen shall come to you.

Think, while you are awake early in the night watches of the most innocent face you ever beheld. Look at it as long as you can face it. This will take you back to the country of purity from whence you came forth. Elisha took the salt of innocence and healed the barren land and water where the theological school was established. They had been looking at sin. He turned their thoughts to inno cence. *"The pure in heart see God."* (Matthew 5:8) This is rest. God is rest. "He rested." A new truth will arise with the innocent every morning.

Inter Ocean Newspaper, January 7, 1894

LESSON II

Adam's Sin and God's Grace

Genesis 3:1-15

The judgment day has arrived when all men have equally good judgment. — C.S.

Why did God make Satan? He did not make him. He permitted him in order that there might be angels excelling in strength. There can be no victories without battles — Peloubet's Select Notes, p.20.

Where did God get Satan to permit? Let us have good judgment.

Jesus Christ called Satan a liar and the father of lies. Then if Satan says, "I am," he lies. If he says, "I was," he lies. If he says, "God permitted me," he lies, and whoever tells such stuff is like unto him. By this process of reasoning we are metaphysically free from Satan. That is we are mentally free. Tell a child there is an invisible Satan prowling around, and the child will some day or night see some shape made visible which will be its formulated ideal of badness. (Vide Luther and the Wesleys.) The lie has passed from your mind to the child's mind and come out as a black man with horns.

Tell the child there is no Satan and there never was any, and the child will never see one. For mind never experiences anything it does not name. The eyes and nerves never feel anything their manager has not named and described.

"Charge some that they teach no other doctrine except of Jesus Christ", said Paul. (1 Timothy 1:3)

"Neither give heed to fables which minister questions rather than godly edifying." (I Timothy 1:4)

Fable of the Garden

If there ever was a fable that ministered questions to mankind it was that one about the good and Wise God's creating Satan and the primeval pair in Eden.

"The flesh profiteth nothing," said Jesus Christ. Why? Because all flesh is but the outward product of language.

This third chapter of Genesis, to which our attention is called, is a lesson in speech and its fruits. The Lord God is the law of the good as it affects matter and evil. While our language is occupied with good and evil there will always be the hope extended of a time when good is victorious. The Adam nature of man calls good evil and evil good. He complained of Eve, who was his gift of

God. Eve complained of her own gift of reasoning whereby she should know that God was all and Satan was nothing.

In the fullness of time, her reasoning should break out as a science of God, which should bruise all evil out of the world. That time is now.

He who complains of his best friends is playing at Adams game. He is arranging arduous tasks for himself. He who complains of the reasoning faculty is playing at Eve's game. He is arranging great physical agony for himself. Look out for sickness.

Looked for Sympathy

Both Adam and Eve complain of not having enough and being enough. They thought they ought to be sympathized with. Whoever is looking for sympathy is playing at the game of Adam and Eve. Whoever sympathizes is playing at the serpent's game. But it is a fable from beginning to end because the pair that God made and pronounced "good" were incapable of actually experiencing the Adam and Eve nonsense.

There is a divine spark of lightning from the true God in every creature. It never gets entangled with the talk that formulates Satan, hard work, or sickness. It has been surrounded by this talk for ages, but never has paid any attention to it.

He who studies Adam, Eve, Satan, may get mixed into their quality if he likes and institute a manner of getting out of the maze. He may keep himself free from it if he pleases by knowing them as nothing at all.

He may think that some time they will be gone or he may think they will be eternal. "Matter is eternal," says one. "It is the shadow that is lost in spirit," says another.

"We shall have to throw away this pottage," said the students at Gilgal. But Elisha put meal into the pottage and it was healed of its poison.

"The time for the deliverance of man from the clutches of Adam is slow," say the people. But whoever knows there was no Adam and knows that the whole story is a fable is exempt now, to-day, from everything Adam and Satan are supposed to have blocked us into. The healing meal for the poison of time is one truth. Think it over carefully and see how quickly you will be set free. "Adam and Eve and Satan are the fable of the language of good and evil with reward and punishments named instead of fruit of lips."

The True Doctrine

This is right doctrine. What is your judgment of it? What you think about it runs into it at right angles or diagonally at an acute angle and will strike fire. If it seems true and reasonable a strong demonstration will take place. An entirely new event will transpire which will please you greatly.

If you cannot accept it no such event will take hold of you.

To "eat of the fruits of the trees of the garden except one" is to know all about good and nothing about evil. Reasoning teaches that the word if evil will seem to fruit if the word of good is capable of fruiting. God the divine intelligence knows that neither good nor evil is reality.

Reasoning would keep mind harping on the law of cause and effect, both good and evil. God, the divine intelligence spark would have none of either cause or effect.

A contradiction of evil is as eye-opening as a contradiction of good. Disputing causes to look two ways at once. That true God is straight ahead.

The good always determines what is evil and what shall happen to evil. So God, the good, represented as showing Adam and Eve and the serpent what comes of their disputing the good. "To talk of evil is to die." "To talk of good is to live." But there is neither death nor life for the divine unquenchable lightning spark. It is exempt from such logical reasonings.

He who has, as Adam, got into the meshes of believing that hunger and poverty and sickness are real, will sit on the side of a good reasoning and praise of the good till he arrives into experiencing happiness. Then he will realize that happiness is real only just long enough to forget all misery. As it is prophesied: *"They shall forget misery."* (Proverbs 31:7) He will next call bliss as unreal as misery. He will then behold God. *"The pure in heart see God."* (Mathew 5:8) No happy man is pure enough to behold God, as no unhappy man is pure enough. The lightning spark is non-conformist.

It sees God without the pull of good and without the cramp of evil. It is God itself.

Concentrate all attention toward it and you see yourself as you are. In truth you are it.

Inter-Ocean Newspaper, January 14, 1894

LESSON III

Cain and Abel

Genesis 4:3-13

A Prussian physician discovered that there is a region within every man that is not sick, no matter how sick a man may seem to be. Religion is based on the discovery that there is a region within every man that is not sinful, no matter how contemptibly a man may perform.

Mocking is a great principle. It is sometimes spoken of as imitation. We certainly do grow to look and act like the people and conduct we observe around us. Then we radiate a quality about us, which other people and even objects assimilate.

The Shinto teachers tell their ministers never to look at their audiences in order that they may not be distracted from looking at their own thoughts. We are able to look at a thought as steadily as at a person. And afterward we as certainly appear and perform like that thought as we appear and perform like the people we look at.

The Prussian physician kept his eye on the region in his patients where they were wholesome. This restored them to health. Jesus kept his eye on the sinless region of those who followed him constantly, and this restored their whole character to nobility.

Some men keep their mind's eye perpetually on the poverty and mournfulness of this planet. Such men diffuse gloom and discouragement unconsciously. They are called philanthropists and reformers. Keep away from them. Keep them off your premises, unless you have the secret of Jesus concerning contagion. His secret was the art of keeping the mind's eye on the joyous and merry department within even the "reformers' mind.

> *"That thou seest*
>
> *That thou beest."*

This department is irresistibly contagious. It is omnipotent. It is perfection. It is the soul region. It is the God in man. Whoever talks about Adam and Eve and Cain is not looking at the soul region of the human race. Whoever talks about Jesus Christ is looking at the soul region of the human race.

Types of the Race

The book of Genesis exhibits all the regions of the race mind under the titles of Jubal, Tubal-Cain, Lamech, Abel, and so on. We are asked to notice such men today as are named in Genesis 4. Each one represents a streak in every man's make up as well as in the race mind *in toto*.

It is self-evident truth when we say "God is indestructible, unchangeable, spirit." It is reasonable to say: "The God in man is his undiscourageable, undefilable center." It is common sense to state that if there is such a region in each street-sweeper, it is wise to find out the method for exposing it. It is the province of science to proclaim that the Abel, Cain, Adah, Zillah regions, or streaks of man are not his indestructible and undiscourageable soul. They are "the shadow systems gathered round the me."

Therefore when I discuss Cain and Abel, I discuss shadows. If I get sorry for the murdered Abel or "righteously indignant" at Cain, who "slew him," I am wound up in shadows. If there is a science that can enable one to look at fools and thieves and know that they are not real and never were real, that must be the ethical science man is searching after.

The forty children of Bethel saw only the baldheadedness of Elisha. They mocked it. That is, they imitated his belief in old age and hugged them to death. God never has baldheadedness leading to decrepitude and the cemetery. The God region in Elisha was immortal youth and deathless strength. These young people should have been as careful to see the young and beautiful godhood of Elisha as the Prussian physician was to see the undefilable health of his patients.

God in the Murderer

The fourth Genesis causes a young man to ask many questions concerning God and man that his teachers are either obliged to hush him up or come right out with the truth of the case and call it a parable of the way thoughts act when men believe in the shadow system as a reality.

Where did Cain get his murdering ability? From Adam. Who was Adam? Nobody. Did not he ever live? No.

Have we not all an Adam nature, *"prone to err as the sparks to fly upward?"* (Job 5:7) No. How can you say that when appearances all show that way? So does the sun appear to rise in the east, but it does nothing of the kind. Don't you believe that any man ever murdered his fellow man? No. What were Guiteau and Prendergast? Nothing. How can you be so ridiculously foolish when our wisest scholars prove that they were criminally wicked people? Because, like the Prussian physician with his eye on the wholesome region, and like Jesus with his eye on the soul of the thief on the cross, I must keep my eye on the God in Guiteau and Prendergast. If I put my eye on the streaks they will increase. If I put my eye on the light, it will light the whole world. I must be "one pointed," as the Brahmins taught, or "single eyed" as Jesus taught. I must not mind what the masters and scholars upon the earth teach, for *"the Lord will cut off both the master and the scholar"* (Malachi 2:12) that give their mind up to the acknowledging evil, while the "simplest man who in his integrity worships (or sees only) God," becomes God.

If I am to manifest what I see in you, I prefer to see God in you now and forever. Then Cain is only a myth. He is just a statement of how mixed up and unhappy a mind is that lets itself see itself as less wonderful than it is. As soon as you or I see ourselves as less wonderful, less capable, less beautiful than we are, we are Cain. It is a destructive sight. As soon as we admit that we are partly wise and partly foolish, sometimes good and sometimes bad, we are Abel. When our great men; so called, tell us that God has made some people to be beautiful and some to be ugly, some brilliant and some dull, they are Cain. When we agree with them, we are Abel. We get rubbed out with discouragement and they stay on *among men with their Tubal-Cains. "artificers in brass and iron" (Verse 22), and their Jubal-Cains, "musicians and philosophers." (Verse 21)*

God Nature Unalterable

We can play with our Cain and Abel myths for 6,000 years, if we like, but it will not defile or alter our God nature. But as 6,000 years of looking at unreality is quite long enough to play with shadows, we now rise in our Jesus Christ reality and proclaim that *God in man as all there is of man all there ever was of him, and all there ever will be of him.* (Genesis 1)

17

Within each living creature is "one who knows." That is the one who dares. It is that one who knows he cannot be slain, and he cannot slay. Shall I be interested in the foolish and cowardly while the steady glory of that everlasting nobility is shining on my face from the immortal heights of every creature's soul telling me "if I see it, I be it," and that is lofty wisdom to be it and the visibility of Jesus Christ to acknowledge it?

Whether this word reach the outer ears of the multitude or this doctrine strike their outer sight makes no difference. The mental breezes waft its saving truth into the universal heart, where judgment sits on, her eternal throne. It does not need recognition by external man; it is already being smiled upon by the true man of God dwelling in all men.

Inter-Ocean Newspaper January 21, 1894

LESSON IV

God's Covenant with Noah

Genesis 9:8-17

Myths and Bible stories depict the state of each man's mind under the dominion of some one or other idea. The Greek allegory of Amor and Psyche teaches the redemption of intuition from the emotions. The story of Elijah and Elisha teaches the effect of peaceableness set free from sternness.

Viewed in this way they all become excellent directions in the practice of what the theosophists call "Raja Yoga," or right handling of thoughts.

From Sankyha philosophy to astrologers' "charms," religion and ethics are struggling to instruct men how to attain beatitude, or exemption from every sort of ill. Religion seems to have "given up the ship" of expectation that exemption from misery is possible this side the tomb. The pulpit assures me that "man is born to trouble."

It is written of the worm that at the least pressure it turns. It is recorded of Mary that once she

19

did something on her own responsibility. She had always faithfully obeyed Martha till that day. It is told of Abel's blood that it is talking up its rights. It was not till Elijah was "cut off from the head" of obedient Elisha that Elisha fed a famished city, increased corn and loaves, raised the dead, watered thirsty armies, and defended himself from enemies by peaceful, peaceable, unrevengeful spiritual qualities, quite unlike his master's explanation of how miracles were wrought. The schools of Gilgal and Jericho understood that the reign of violence and vengefulness must give place eventually to spiritual mercifulness. The students of both schools told Elisha that, *"This day must thy master (Elijah), be cut from thy head."* (2 Kings 2:3) This is one of the very few 'instantaneous treatments" given in religious "Raja Yoga."

Jesus Christ gave one: *"Now is the accepted time."* (2 Corinthians 6:2) Millions of Christians have pounded on that treatment, denied it, explained it away, pointed to the state of the world and argued from hope, but here it is, just as simple, just as true as ever, "Now is the accepted time."

Value of Instantaneous Action

We have thousands of people striking and stamping theological proposition that "this day shall doing the work of the universe by stern effort be cut off from the head of church of the spirit, but here are the enemies of the globe standing still and the looms and traffic of creation idle because

20

that treatment has gone forth with its irresistible demonstrableness. John Webster said: "Strike while the iron is hot."

Thousands, yea millions, have hurried and scurried to find the right instant to strike on their affairs to accomplish their purposes because his mind was strong and compelled them to think as he told them.

But there is another story to tell of the cold iron of your human lot as it enters into your heart today, the result of the strife and struggle of your past. You can strike that iron with the hammer of some simple truth it is white hot with joyousness.

Noah saw the rainbow setting its seven-hued arch against the cloud-curtained eastern sky. To all the inhabitants of his world it meant that a storm had come and gone, with death and terror on its wings, and might so come and go again. He set up his protest. He rose away from the man of affairs as the man of rest, and so spoke once from his own instinct. His name meant "rest." When he wrote with the pen of his own genius across the face of one item of nature's proud caravan, it responded with glad obedience. Noah's resurrection of his own native genius has testified that the rainbow stands an everlasting promise that the waters shall never cover the earth again but shall stay in their appointed basins till the heavens be dissolved and the mountains are no more.

The Lessons of the Rainbow

This is the lesson we are told in Genesis, 9:8-17. Noah rose from his hiding place. Rest rose from its brow-beaten darkness. Noah had obeyed struggle, effort, brave persistence. This was not his native talent. Drowning, crying, despairing were the fruits of rest being kept out of sight and struggle put foremost.

Within every mind is the Noah quality. If it is given freedom it marks every object with divine kindness. Nothing from thenceforth hath power to hurt. Leonardo da Vinci, sitting motionless before the altar cloth till his Noah quality was set free, painted something to the lasting story of the power of the spirit.

"In returning and rest shall ye be saved; in quietness and confidence shall be your strength." (Isaiah 30:15)

On the cold, hard want of this age there are some unnamed lovers of the doctrine of meekness, softly but commandingly printing a principle seven times heated with its own dissolving might. As the spirit of gentleness was Elisha's miracle worker, and it wrought no wonders for the world till the stern rigors of Elijah were taken away from mastership over him; as Noah's genius for command could only rise after the stormy terrors of cursing had had full sway, so not till the mind of man has ceased to look for prosperity by worldly struggle and competitions may the gentle doctrine of Jesus be seen as able by its own utterance to do all things that mind can ask.

There is no practice more successful than letting myself be myself, for at its edict it is meant that nature shall bend the knee. There is that within every man that is opposed to war and competition. It is the Noah quality. It is the stillness of the changeless divinity which in this lesson is called Noah talking with God.

When we hang on the dark skies of misfortune the true doctrine of Jesus, they shine with the promise that misfortune shall never deluge our mind and life forevermore.

"If a man keep my sayings he shall never see death," (John 8:51-52) of peace or joy. There is no handling of thoughts can equal these sayings. They undo the practices that have hitherto prevailed over man, subtly, noiselessly, easily. They usher in exemption from every ill. They make God visible.

Inter-Ocean Newspaper January 28, 1894

LESSON V

Beginning of the Hebrew Nation

Genesis 12:1- 9

Golden Text; "I will bless thee and make thy name great; and thou shalt be a blessing." (Verse 2)

Mozart said in his letters that whenever he saw a grand mountain or a wonderful piece of scenery it said to him, "Turn me into music; play me on the organ." So whenever one who is devoted to the mind principle reads the Bible stories he immediately sets the historic characters to some mental quality and reads the book of some man's fate backward and forward. He who has for his ruling mind trait the Abram quality will find himself moved up and away from his neighbors.

Was not Anaxagoras banished for teaching that there is one divine mind acting upon the universe with intelligence and design? "Abram" means "exalted father." Whoever has one high theme that occupies his mind as truth in the midst of a society satisfied with lower themes will be assured by his own inner consciousness, or reassured by some unusual phenomenon formulated for his sake, that the lofty theme shall some day have a multitude of followers. *"And I will make of thee a great nation."* (Verse 2)

The Abram theme that is rising now in the mind of society as the founder of a universal nation is this: "There is only God." It is as ostracizing to you to hold this theme in your confidence today if you attempt to express it and specify as it was for Abram, B.C. 1921, to proclaim: "There is but one God." For society, judging after the sight of the eyes and the hearing of the ears, still holds, as Ur of old, that many principles rule our world besides changeless harmony. Some start up from the bottomless deeps of their imagination the proposition that there is disease occupying space and spot, and where he holds his red and black carnivals, there is no sign of the kindness of God. Some reel forth the fanciful yarn of a ruler called "want," whose reign it is the struggle of their life to undo. They cannot agree with what the Abram doctrine exalting itself in the mind of many Christians today. So the Christians' crowning glory, their noblest truth, the coming faith of the world, "departeth as the Lord commandeth" into the silent regions where the new people shall be born whose religion shall rule the earth.

No Use For Other Themes

When the Abram theme gets to ruling there is no use for any other theme to set up its claim. A man will keep silent if he believes God is all, but he will not descend to believe in anything else after he has felt the buoyant winds of that truth bearing him up on their pinions, thrilling him with their promises.

We read in Japanese religious myths what a clinch Bimbogami has on the actions of a man when he gets uppermost in his mind. Bimbogami means the idea of poverty. We have seen Bimbogami get uppermost as an idea in millions of minds. We see how destitution and despair show forth as the fruitage of the theme called poverty. But this lesson shows what follows, having for an uppermost theme: "There is but one." Jesus Christ said it was a prospering theme. "Ye shall have a hundred fold more in this life." It promised Abram "great name, great power, great blessings."

The theme, "There is only God," promises absolute immunity from hardship. It goes as an army of protection before the man who holds it. *"Be not afraid, I have overcome the world."* (John 16:33) It furnishes him his home and his comrades. *"I go to prepare a place for you."* (John 14:2) It goes as merciful motherhood. *"I will send the Comforter."* (John 14:16) It comes as wonderful wisdom, touching pen with subtle fires and tongue with irresistible lightnings. *"The Holy Ghost shall teach you all things."* (John 14:26)

It promises the ends of the earth for an audience. *"I am with you even to the end of the world."* (Matthew 28:20) It may look quite the contrary for many days and nights to the Abram quality of today when it sets up its rule. Poverty and deformity may set up their tabernacles on your premises if your heart has liberated the Abram doctrine of our age, *"but every knee shall bow and every tongue confess"* (Philippians 2:10-11) that it is the right doctrine.

Have you not read how the promise, *"I will make thy name great,"* (Genesis 12:2) was fulfilled so perfectly to Abram that no man has ever yet been so widely and so permanently honored, since both Mohammedans and Jews, equally with Christians, honor the name and character of Abraham? Have you not read how he was prosperous on every plane, fulfilling the decrees of right doctrine, that on no plane shall there be destitution when one gives it the ruling of his destiny?

Influence of Noble Themes

Do you suppose there are beggars in the kingdom where noble themes are regnant? Do you suppose there are crimes in the realm where the science of Christ is understood? Thus does one who perceives how it works with a man to give free reign to his most exalted theme call attention to the thinking principle. "If you can manage your draughts, your stove will broil and bake to perfection," says the stove man. "If you can manage your talking, your body will perform to perfection," says

28

the man who, by talking to his body, gets it to performing great feats. "If you can handle your thoughts, you can fill the convolutions of your brain with sparkling globules of that gray matter so beloved by great thinkers," says the thought wind as it blows past our heads, entering only where our mind doors are open. "If you will let an exalted theme be your only theme, it will lift you out of the depths; it will buoy you over the breakers; it will waft you on wings of glory; God shall wipe away your tears; angels shall feed and clothe you; Jesus Christ will work miracles for you wherever you walk." There is only God to him who knows it is true that there is only God.

Abram should not have "taken Lot along with him" till he had transmuted Lot's quality from clouding and covering his face all the time with inability to see how an exalted principle works. Abram's blind obedience was like the cook's blind obedience to the stove man's directions about draughts. It is possible to see into the principle of draughts. It is possible to see an idea in its workshop. But even those who believe there is only God are lugging along a "Lot" who keeps them from seeing clearly what manner of movements their high truth loves best and keeps them from seeing where their noble truth will fulfill itself.

Danger In Looking Back

The "Lot" which the Abram doctrine is now covered with is the teaching that "there is no God," without the potency within itself to make itself consistent with "there is only God," without a great deal of controversy. It causes its hearers to look back to doctrines exposed on less giddy heights. But having taken these two friendly propositions, none can "look back" without being petrified as Lot's wife.

"Sarah" is the only companion "Abram need take," which means that whoever holds the principle clearly that there is only God, will have the name "Jesus Christ" woven into it and with it till its hidden potency shall break forth. *"I know thy works, and where thou dwellest, and thou holdest fast my name,"* (Revelation 2:13) and *"I will give thee a white stone, and in the stone a new name."* (Revelation 2:17) *"And the Lord said unto Abram, Unto thy seed will I give this land."* (Verse 7) The name that accompanies the "exalted father" is "Prince of Peace," as Sarai was Princess of the Home. Having them in thy heart, "there shall no ill come nigh thy dwellings."

"And Abram journeyed, going on still toward the south." (Verse 9) "The south" is a figure of speech for warmth, gladness, harmony, beauty, wisdom. Those who have the one and only regnant principle of today already can sight the white promontories of New Canaan's happy shores.

Inter-Ocean Newspaper February 4, 1894

LESSON VI

God's Covenant With Abram

Genesis 17: 1-9

Two angels accompany every one of us from alpha to omega. Their names are Peace and Happiness. One is never realized without the presence of the other. These two angels are to the mind what the eyes are to the head, for they behold what lies before and show what is the right path. It is written of little children that "their angels do always behold the face of the father." The father is God. When the child looks into its mother's face it sees only God. When it no longer sees God in its mother's face, it is no longer a child.

When a child feels the sunshine of God's face hot and wonderful, we remark of it that it is a genius. Every genius had once some way of being happy and peaceful long enough to feel the sunshine of the face of God on its face. Thus, Paganini, while yet a boy, astonished Italy with his music. Thus, the Genoese traveler and his genius for discovering new lands pushed him out over stormy waters safely to the yellow sands of the free new West.

Humboldt wrote in the register of a mountain hotel, "Citizen of the World." Jesus Christ wrote on the pages of the summit wisdom of all time, "Citizen of Heaven." He had a genius for finding heavenly places and seeing heavenly sights everywhere. The cripple never looked crippled to him. He saw in his face the face of God, and saith unto him, "One is your Father." The sinner never looked sinful, the leper was not repulsive, the prisoner was forever free in his eyes. "The kingdom of God is within you."

As Little Children

Is it possible, after having seen sinners and beggars, to return again into a childhood's vision which sees only God? We are under orders to "become as little children." Abram had an "H" from Jehovah's own name, and Sarai also received the mark of the child in her forehead and became Sarah. The disciples of Jesus became wise in discovering the perfections of man. Wherever their eyes fell on people and things, they showed forth their godhood.

People who abide in peace accomplish more miracles than the strivers and strainers. *"Abram believed in the Lord, and it was accounted to him for righteousness!"* (Genesis 15:6) "The Lord" is the self of man. The more a man believes in himself the more good he sheds abroad. He often looks through peace and happiness into the face of God.

32

He makes no effort to convert the heathen when he sees the goodness and holiness of the Father in their faces.

It is possible to be such a genius at sighting goodness and wisdom in the faces of men that it would be accounted a subtle species of stealing on my part if I were to aver that any one of them was a heathen or reprobate. It is possible to be such a genius at sighting the knowledge of God in man's hearts that it would be accounted a species of stealing on my part if I were to proclaim that they ought to have missionaries to teach them God.

"He who filches from me my good name

Doth that which not enriches him nor any man."

If every man on the earth would often tell what he honestly believed in his own self, he would soon begin to show forth his innate greatness. Does he verily believe in his own integrity? Let him tell himself this truth often within his own soul. Does he believe in his own ability? Let him acknowledge it in so many words to himself. Does he believe that he is in the right in that which he calls his religion? Let him affirm that he is in the right.

God and Mammon

No man ever felt any soul rest except in what he honestly believed himself to be. This is called his own "bed" in our Bible. *"Take up thy bed and go thy way."* (Matthew 9:6) The time when one takes an honest survey of what he does believe, is after he has been struggling on some line, which has not accomplished anything. Do you believe that God clothes you, or do you believe that money clothes you? Could you travel from Chicago to New York without money? Could you have a mouthful to eat without money? What are you working for? Do you wonder that some people have affirmed that money is God?

As a people making money our god, we have reached our bitter extremity. Of such it is written, *"The prayer of faith shall save, and God shall raise him up at the last day."* (John 6:4) "Abram was ninety and nine," (Verse 1) and no signs of a son through whom to propagate himself had been given. Then he made a new covenant. As our world has arrived at its 99th percent of trouble, let it now, before it tastes its 100th percent thereof — which is starvation, make its covenant with its God. When a man tells what he believes, he is making a covenant with a principle. The principle he tells himself he honestly believes in is the one that will work with him. *"I am Almighty God. Walk before me and be thou perfect."* (Verse 1)

If, when you tell what you honestly believe, you feel happiness and peace in any degree, you are then beholding the face of God, and it will surely be a "treatment" which will stimulate your native genius. Your own greatness will come forward. As you are truly greater than circumstances and environments, no matter how powerful they may seem to be, it is right for you to know it. To

Abram, 1,900 years before Jesus, his own worthiness was so real to him that it spoke audibly.

Being Honest With Self

His own greatness, goodness, worthiness was his God. If money is your God it will do you good to acknowledge it to yourself and talk to your money face to face. The main proposition of today's lesson is: Be honest with yourself as to what you believe is good in yourself and what you believe it is good for you to have. This honesty will begin a new base for you to operate upon. A new base is an excellent thing. Taken after the order and direction of this lesson, thou mayest be confident that *"kings shall come out of thee."* (Verse 6)

The people have been slyly believing in money as their dependence, but outwardly proclaiming God the invisible spirit as their support. This has made a slimy basis. Now they face themselves up and begin again. This is strength, discovery of new powers, inspiration. And in our chapter now before us, inspiration and greatness are called "kings."

When a pietist after the Guyon, Fenelon type of abusing his body, calling himself a monkey, reviling the world, calling it a snare and wickedness, faces himself up he will ask, "Why am I teaching myself to hate the outer world and my body, whose house of abiding I find myself in? Within me do I hate or love them?" He will say, "I love them. I believe they are beautiful and comfortable till I abuse them and revile them. The people are lovely to me till I strike them with the lash of my will-trained tongue."

Immediately, the pietist will begin a new base. This will be "a new covenant."

It is the exquisite honesty of the child that makes it so free, so wise, so beautiful. It is its honesty that causes its two angels to face the true God and illuminate it with genius. He who is honest with himself, telling what quality he believes he has and what he believes is good for him to have, starts as a little child. Thus, Isaac was promised to Abram.

When we have practiced telling ourselves what we do believe, we shall find certain results have started themselves going in our character. These are called "generations" in the 9th verse. By "generations," we always understand the Bible to signify "results." Theosophists call results by the title "karma."

In pure character lessons, as related to environments, which is our ministry, we see the "results" of taking up our "bed" or faith, or making a new base, which is making a covenant, which is confessing our honest confidence.

Let us mention some character "generations" which Abram saw would be "everlasting possessions" to us.

     a) We shall be exactly what we pretend to be;

b) We shall be controllers of matter, not controlled by it;

c) No physical conditions can disturb the equilibrium of our mind;

d) We shall not need the favor of anybody to make us happy; we shall be above craving for love, sympathy or praise;

e) We shall appreciate our own unchanging divinity.

Inter-Ocean Newspaper February 11, 1894

LESSON VII

God's Judgment of Sodom

Genesis 18:22-33

There is a saying ascribed to Matthias (that apostle who took the place of Judas and was martyred in Ethiopia) which reads, "If the neighbor of an elect man sin, the elect man sinned himself."

There is a saying of Jesus, which reads, *"The kingdom of heaven (within you) is like unto leaven."* (Matthew 13:33) Said Alexander Dumas, "When man is no longer afraid of death for himself and no longer causes the death of his neighbor, then man is God."

Abraham, in this 18th Chapter of Genesis is practicing concentration of mind upon the power of righteousness. He fastens his mental gaze upon Sodom and struggles to see the ability of a less and less quantity of leaven to leaven the whole lump thereof. He sees that the least number of men agreeing upon one principle that can cause a large city to agree with them is ten.

The recognition of the right of all men to equal freedom from bondage of any kind, if held firmly by ten men in a city, causes all that city to recognize the right.

The recognition of the spiritual substance moving in all men, if held steadfastly by ten men in a city, will make all that city finally acknowledge that one force alone animates them, and that is Spirit.

Pantalaji, the Hindu sage, said: "By concentrating the mind upon minute, concealed or distant objects in every department of nature, one may acquire thorough knowledge concerning them."

The soul, the spirit, the divine spark, may seem minute, concealed, distant, in our neighbor, but if by concentrating our mind upon it we may cause it to stand forth, is it not worth practicing concentration to accomplish?

Abraham drew forth one man whom the intrepid Peter pronounces "righteous," although history describes him as the reverse. He had not the strength of gaze to see ten men, all of like mind with himself. The city looked too dark with sinfulness, but his faithful effort accomplished better than he planned.

The White Cross Legion had a motto, which was significant of the leavening power of mind focused to one pure principle, "My strength is as the strength of ten, because my heart is pure." It

has had a wonderful influence on public senti-
ment. The best motives of tens of thousands of
men have stood forth, and the baser have been
forgotten, as Lot was all that was left of Sodom.

No Right Nor Wrong In Truth

Take the Bible stories as personifying mind,
moral quality, and abstract principles. Abraham is
mind closing round the noble truth that God is all.
The statement is new, and all appearances of nature and human kind dispute it. While it is yet a
new statement, and Sodom has not yet been per-
meated with it, that other truth is made apparent,
viz., that there is in truth neither right nor wrong.
In truth, there are no descriptions of opposites.

Abraham willingly saw Lot as the only righteous man in Sodom. So if I feel secure and strong
in the might of my wonderful principle that God is
all there is, I become fearless to say that as my
idea of God has been my God, I am glad to let go
all my ideas for truth itself to have free transit
through me. Now it is plain that the world which
feels so divided between fear of virtue and fear of
vice can only be rid of its double fear by my saying
into its face that, in the spirit of the universe,
there is no virtue for the viceful to fear and no vice
for the virtuous to fear.

Thus Lot stands forth, who seems to darken
and to hide the glory of the young recognition that
God is all, filling the sands with his substance,
and the scorpions with his goodness. For Lot is
utterly indifferent to virtue and vice, pain and

peace, right and wrong. He does not claim to be righteous or wicked. He is an impersonal, unformulated statement of the principle, willing to be the skill of the forger and of the detective, praised by Peter, scolded by Calvin, raining on the just and on the unjust alike, drowning the mission ship "Morning Star" and the pirate boat all in one breath by their both alike believing in Satan and Jesus: one fearing Jesus, the other fearing Satan.

Shall not the fear principle operate according to its own regular method? And is it any wonder that mankind finds Lot a mysterious character? And is it not plain that the truth that now flows so freely through the channels made by the glorified First Principle is a mystery to all but those who are as open for abstract truth to flow unhindered by their preconceived ideas as Abraham? What a mystery is the truth that there is neither right nor wrong in truth!

Among the sayings of Jesus in common use among the primitive Christians was this: "Beholding one working on the Sabbath, he saith unto him, "Man, if thou knowest what thou doest, blessed art thou; but if thou knowest not, accursed art thou, and a transgressor of the law."

Ezekiel, prophesying of this doctrine when it should spring forth in these days as a mental science, wrote: "I will cut off from thee the *righteous and the wicked, saith the Lord.*" (Ezekiel 21:3)

Misery Shall Cease

There is no thought we can let stream through us more dematerializing than the Lot thought. And it is the explanation of all Sodom or all this planet. Principle is principle. Attend unto it and agree with it, that there shall be no pain and the very knowledge of pain may leave the planet. Attend unto it and agree with its almightiness, that misery shall cease. Attend unto it and agree with it, that happiness and ease shall not be purchased at the expense of the animals, of the poor, of the helpless.

"He will deliver the needy when he crieth, the poor also, and him that hath no helper."

Goodness that mourns over vice is not goodness. It is double sight. Jesus taught the advantage of single sight. *"Shall not the judge of all the earth do right?"* (Verse 25) asked Abraham. Whatever state of body, mind, surroundings we are now in, this is our judgment. Do not the lines and colors tell the age of a man?

"In whatsoever state I find you, in that I judge you," is now an acknowledged teaching of Jesus. This is right. This is leprosy, beauty, lameness, litheness. This is "karma." What doeth Jesus therewith? Standing in the door of Peter's house, "he suffered not these things to speak," the devils our visions call the karma, which we do not like.

There is nothing so understanding to the institutions of men as the two secret doctrines clearly understood by the Jesus Christ in all men. Do you understand how a man by knowledge could break the Sabbath and not break it? Then you see how Lot could talk and act as he did and purposely be hastening the disappearance of Sodom, as the wisest answer to Abraham's prayers. Abraham found not ten to say, "The God in man is all there is of man." Before he had drawn them out of the shadows by concentrated intention, he saw that his first idea of righteousness was fear and recognition of vice in a subtle form.

The whole city was saved when the mysterious Lot was saved. Fear was burned as chaff. Who built our magnificent churches? Men who feared poverty, hunger, cold, debt. Who built our stately prisons? Men who feared vice, death, pain. What are they all, the cloud-capp'd towers, the solemn temples, the great globe itself?" Sodom the double fear. What shall become of them? Like Sodom, "they shall dissolve, and like its insubstantial pageant, faded, leave not a rack behind." What shall be seen here where the shades of fear are settled on our dear little earth with its little handful of mankind? The countless Elohim who say, "there is only God"; the angelic hosts who know neither good nor evil; "the church of Pergamos which held fast my name" till its new name, not citadel of safety, but neither safety nor danger, was written. *"Behold, I create new heavens and a new earth; and the former shall not be remembered, nor come*

into mind." (Isaiah 65:17) Here are the Abraham,
Lot, Sarah, Isaac, of the universal mind.

Inter-Ocean Newspaper February 18, 1894

LESSONV III

Trial of Abraham's Faith

Genesis 22:1-13

When a man is bound to some old trait of character or prejudice which keeps coming up and interfering with his later principles, we say he is Ixion bound to his wheel. Abraham had been brought up to believe in slaughtering animals to appease the wrath of his God. He had often seen children sacrificed to suit the savage appetites of a watchful and jealous deity. Even after the gleaming majesty of his true relations with the real God had been vouchsafed, he clung to the notion of sacrificing something to curry further patronage from his Jehovah.

So much for simple history on the phenomenal plane of man's early struggles to lift himself from the hypnotism of church, state and school errors. Poor Abraham never unglued himself from the error of cutting up little lambs and calves to gratify the Almighty, and to this day certain of us are still psychologized by the ancient belief that our

45

own life and health are prolonged and improved by
stockyard tragedies. Only the supermost idealism,
persistently preached till the songs of all the angels on all the Moriahs of all men's hearts are the
only sounds heard, can hush the error that —

> *"Life ever more is fed by death,*
>
> *In earth and sea and sky,*
>
> *And that a rose may breathe its breath*
>
> *Something must die."*

While the question stirs the heart of man why
such things should be, there will forever be the
voice from the ideal, which is forever the only real,
that "I will have mercy, and not sacrifice," "He
that killeth an ox is as if he slew a man," and "Lay
not thine hand upon the Lord's anointed."

We are not expected, according to the Jesus
Christ doctrine, to look to these texts of Genesis
from the materialistic standpoint. We need not
trace the history of man's slow awakening from
the ages old hypnotic stupor of that first suggestion to him of how the universe would look and act
if God were not God and the God in man were not
all there is of man.

Light Comes With Preaching

We hear the orders of the merciful and mighty
Jesus Christ, *"What is preached to you in darkness
(parables and Old Testament stories, which are
symbols) that preach ye in the light"* (Luke 12:3) —
which is that there is a real world standing in the

46

midst of all that we are now looking at, and it shall appear in all the splendor of its light by our persistent talk and thought about it.

"We feel its airs blow o'er us,

And a glory shines before us,

Of how 'twas meant to be

With all mankind."

We sometimes hear men of great love and knowledge say that it is not much use to try spiritualizing the race by preaching to grownup men and women. They feel that our only hope is with the children. But they are talking from their sight of darkness. "Preach ye in the light!" commands Jesus Christ.

A horde of men came into the presence of Jesus Christ with a dark claim against a woman, chaining her by their agreement with sin. He said that there should be one without sin to first cast a stone at her. So he himself, the man entirely without sin, did cast a stone at her.

This was the stone he threw: "I see God in you." And all those men who stood for darkness sank into the sands as the light of the world rose on the doctrine of the reality of sin. *"Hath no man condemned thee?"* (John 8:10) he asked of the spotless soul. And the answer of the woman falls like an angel's harp into the fingers of the virgin mother of the coming race: *"No man, Lord."* (John 8:11) And he saith unto her: *"Neither do I condemn thee."* (John 8:11)

47

So the hardened men and women of the world have their uncondemned region, and he who would be the Jesus Christ to a world must see only that region in all the race, children and adults, animals and towering intellects in equal presence.

He who takes the stand that the spotless un-condemned soul of man is all there is of man is Abraham. He who takes this stand has joy born into him and forth from him. This is Isaac. He who still clings to his timorousness, to his first teachings of a personal God demanding more and more effort on his already overstrained life, is Abraham, thinking he must not expect joy yet awhile.

You Can Be Happy NOW

If you feel that you must wait a single minute for your joy, while yet you believe that the idea is the real, you are on Moriah. If you let the voice of your soul sing from its hidden heights on the Jesus Christ doctrine of "Now," you will be happy now. If you still think that though you are happy within your own soul and many blessings are yours, while your neighbors still dwell in ignorance and pain, which you cannot ameliorate, you are sacrificing lambs like Abraham.

Your neighbors are as much in the light as you are yourself. Your neighbors have their communions with their own white godhead as much and as often as you do. You shall not seize them from their free grass plots to bleat with pain on your altar of imagining that God is partial to you, and empowers you to call them unhappy and ignorant.

This is the translation of light on the 22nd of Genesis. The only sacrifice ever sung of in the celestial kingdom here abiding is that song of letting be the un-condemned spirit. Go not forth in mind with a knife to slay ignorance or sin. The only knife is the immortal truth that there is only one reality and it never heard of sin. Expect no provisions of food or instruction for the race, for in soul where the race now dwells, they know no want and they gleam and glow with the wisdom they had in the beginning and which can never be taken away. If this be transcendentalism, then Jesus Christ was a transcendentalist, for this is His doctrine.

Inter-Ocean Newspaper February 25, 1894

LESSON IX

Selling the Birthright

Genesis 25:27-34

The subject of this lesson is "Appetite." Esau was hungry for physical food. Jacob "was hungry for honors.." "Isaac loved Esau because he did eat." "Rebekah loved Jacob" for the same reason.

When a man is hungry for knowledge and ignores his bodily appetites, he speaks slightingly of the Esau type whose eyes glisten as he describes game dinners. When a man loves venison and tripe, he has not a voracious appetite for seeing all living things free and happy. He despises such sentimentality.

Protoplasm is the formless life stuff out of which all things are formed. Socrates or the red ant rears his head hungry from the start to eat up all the other amoebae. Protoplasm is filled with mouths. It is maw. It is the bottomless pit. Each mouth is an amoeba. Let not him that is hungry for the praise of men think himself any better off than he who is hungry for "lentil soup" or pate de fois gras. If he tries to convert his neighbors to his kind of appetite he is only an amoeba trying to swallow his neighbor amoeba.

Let not him who is hungry for information concerning the other world that lies so close to this that the rustling wings of its inhabitants may be heard at midnight, imagine that his appetite is a flick more Godlike than the reformer's hunger to find another den of infamy to groan about.

For God is not hungry for information; neither is He hungry to reform the wicked. God is satisfied. Thus he who has least appetite is nearest Godlike.

The struggle of the amoeba, whether his name be Plato or flea, for food to satisfy himself, is the struggle of all things to be satisfied with fullness as God is now satisfied. *"With thee is fullness of joy."* (Psalms 16:11) Nobody ever had enough to eat of the kind of food he had opened his mouth for. Is the richest woman in the world satisfied with the amount of money she has collected?

"Ye Shall Be Filled"

Did not Esau rest a little and then rise up with an increased stomach capacity? One would think that the man who "holds by universal consent the highest rank among the national philosophers of ancient and modern times," the author of the Principia might have felt some little sense of satisfaction, but no! Listen to his Oliver Twist-like cry for more: "To myself I seem to have been only like a boy playing on the seashore, whilst the great ocean of truth lay all undiscovered before me." Did you ever know of one who had praise enough to please him?

Jesus Christ taught that only one hunger would ever be satisfied. *"Blessed are they that do hunger and thirst after righteousness, for they shall be filled."* (Matthew 5:6) Righteousness means God, the one Spirit. There is an ability in the one Spirit filling heaven and earth with itself to satisfy all creatures who open their mouths with intention to swallow the whole spirit of God. "The Father and I will come and make our abode in you." Then ye shall be filled.

It is easy enough to say that Jacob was mean to take advantage of Esau's hunger to steal his birthright. It is easy enough to say that Jacob showed a lack of trust in the promises of God that he should have the birthright without trickery. It is easy enough to point out Esau's faults. For 3,700 years, historians and moralizers have been clear on the right and wrong of Jacob and Esau.

Let us look at the subject from a less hackneyed premise. When we read of *"Esau despising his birthright"* (Verse 34), we are reading of ourselves ignoring or turning away from some suggestion that is offered to us by a spoken word or secret principle. It is suggested to me that if I know the higher mathematics better than any living being, I shall have all the eyes of all the learning of Christendom turned toward me with admiring wonder. But I don't allow that amoeba in the protoplasmic ocean of void in which suggestions rear their hungry heads to eat me up. I, like Esau, exclaim, *"What profit shall this be to me?"* (Verse 32) I hand over to the Newtons of this age all my ambitions in this line.

So Newton despised me for having no appetite for trigonometry and I despised Newton for having no appetite for seeing all the world healed and transfigured. We are only repeating the Esau-Jacob serio-comedy.

It is all a matter of appetite, you on your hungry ethical plane, I on my hungry bodily plane; he on his hungry-for-money plane, she on her hungry-for-praise plane.

While the everlasting truth abides that God is hungry for nothing. How still the eternal God remains in the presence of folly. How silent the wonderful God keeps in the midst of this ceaseless eating!

The Delusion Destroyed

"O thou unshaken one! By thy favor my delusion is destroyed." For I see that it is all delusion, this chasing around after suggestions to eat, this conniving and twisting to keep from being worsted in the battle for existence. The unshaken one, the satisfied one, says one thing to the gnawing void: *"Look unto me and live."* (Isaiah 45:22)

"With heart that abides in me alone and to nothing else wanders, he, through meditation on the Divine Spirit, goes to it." He who goes to God is filled with God. He is filled. For God is able to fill even the soul.

There is one impartial Will that liveth and dieth not, and in that Will all that which ought to be is. When one is looking without himself to quench his thirst and supply his hunger, he is trying to look without to find God. And if he names the substance he is feeling around after by its right name, he will begin to be better fed. He will say, *"Thy will be done."* (Matthew 26:39)

If one is looking within himself to find the wherewithal to satisfy his appetite, and names what he is searching after by its right name, he will begin to be happier. He will say, "Thy will be done."

For in the impartial Will within me and in the impartial Will without me, which is the One Will, all that which ought to be is, and with that which is I am satisfied.

Ages of ages of naming the things without me and within me by the Adam suggestions of good and evil leave me still hungry.

Ages of naming the beauties and glories of heaven by the Joshua suggestions leave me still hungry. But one point of time shorter than the fraction of a second of sight and taste of the will of the Impartial One makes me God. I am awake and am satisfied.

The Adam man names both good and evil. The Joshua man names only good. He complains against nothing. The Jesus Christ man names neither good nor evil. He eats the Impartial Will, and is that Will. It makes its abode in him. We are like what we eat, on whatever plane we are feeding ourselves — Gentile, if Gentiles; moral, if morals; God, if God.

Inter-Ocean Newspaper March 4, 1894

LESSON X

Jacob at Bethel

Genesis 28:10-22

"Truth is thy star of destiny,

And if thou hast truth enough

To render thee a lofty-thoughted, honest man,

Thou hast enough to command The light of ages,

The influence of armies, The fate of empires.

Nothing shall to thee too early come,

Nothing too late;

God is thy fate."

David wrote: *"In thy majesty ride prosperously because of truth."* (Psalms 45:4) But we must not imagine that anything whatsoever that we know of matter is truth. We have many statements concerning matter, but no one has looked majestic or felt majestic because of them. On the contrary, the student of insects who is quoted as authority on antennae invariably gets to looking like the coleoptera he knows most about. Chicago's specialist on carbuncles died of a most revolting one. You may count upon being bone of bone and sinew of sinew of what you are giving your attention unto. You look and act exactly like it.

All the health you have, all the nobility you have, all the intelligence you have, is what you believe of truth. If you have a bad disposition, are quick tempered, arbitrary, selfish, stingy, deceitful, it will not count anything against you if you are positive that one single beautiful proposition you ever heard concerning God is true and have paid good attention to it. That one statement is equal to defrauding your disposition of its prey at the very moment when the moral law would carefully explain you ought to be receiving its consequences.

Many Who Act Like Jacob

There is a large body of people now who would be beggars and sick if they had their desserts, according to the moral law. They have performed with their neighbors and brethren exactly like Jacob performed with Esau. But they have said with great confidence that God fills heaven and earth with his own substance, and there is none other substance anywhere. This mystic principle has worked through their environments like leaven. Today they are buoyed up and mysteriously provided for.

Jacob had one truth with which his destiny was wrought out to some measure of nobility and upon which he rode somewhat prosperously. It was this: "The Lord God brought it to me."

Even when he was stealing his father's blessing, he boldly insisted concerning the little kids which he had just killed, that the Lord God brought them to him to serve unto his father a savory dinner.

Truth is a well of water springing up. It is the Beersheba spot in each man's mind. Jacob lived with Isaac at Beersheba. He had a sneak-thief disposition, which ran him into dark hours, but he had truth enough to revive and cheer him every time. "Man's extremity is God's opportunity." "God is truth."

Jacob had not paid attention enough to his one truth to make him honest and lofty-minded every moment. One ought to notice the absolute truth continually if he would be so noble-thoughted and sincere that all knowledge, all influence, all fate, should be his own without any dark hours or sandy spots.

How to Seek Inspiration

There's many a theory concerning the stones, but there's no inspiration in stones as stones. Inspiration is in the well in the heart of the stone. If you are searching after knowledge you must search into the "ego" of the stone, or into its "well." The trees that lie softly on yon horizon beds of misty sky have somewhat wherewith to revive your drooping hours besides acorns and apples. If you are wise in trees, but do not know their reviving songs, you have wandered into "Haran," and are growing old and stiff like their shaggy barks. If you know their mystic wells and how to drink therefrom, you ride majestically on their buoyant qualities.

The story of Jacob is always the story of the church as it has performed and does perform and ever will perform till it proclaims where Jesus Christ, the living inspiration of the Almighty, truly is.

Has not the church a habit of hiring its pulpit to give it great nobility among the inhabitants of earth? When the church buys the minister's services, the church is buying Esau's birthright of free speech. The pulpit orator has always been "Esau." The church has always been "Jacob." We all know right well that "Esau" (that is, the minister) has to preach exactly what his audiences like, regardless of whether it is true or not, else he and his family may go hungry. So "Esau," who cannot bear to go hungry, whose heart would faint to see his children on the street, sells his birthright of free speech, and Jacob (the church) wanders to this day in "Haran" (which means "dry"). It is from the congregation (which is the "Jacob" of the church) that all privilege to express new ideas springs. Then as the church gives its gold and silver and good shelter (lentil soup) to its "Esau" in exchange for what the preacher really does believe, Jacob, the congregation, will have spells of seeing "angels," of hearing "promises," and trying to bargain with the very Lord Jehovah himself to take care of their prosperity if they "*will give one-tenth thereof to him.*" (Verse 22)

When Esau gives all his birthright freely forth, Jacob will not attempt to force the everlasting God down to accepting one-tenth of his earnings, one-tenth of his time, one-tenth of his heart.

Christ, the True Pulpit Orator

Jesus Christ was the genuine pulpit orator. He gave forth from the well within him regardless of whether the congregations furnished him with sandals or not. He taught plainly that his church must give all it had — all it had, each member of it — all its time to studying God; all its attention to watching God; all its heart to God. Nothing was said by him about selling pews to help pay for his dinners, nothing deferential in him to the man who put in one-tenth; he rather spoke boldly that the woman who put in all she had was drinking of the well he was drinking from, though she put in only one-fifth of a cent.

If you have truth enough to cause you to give your palatial doors wide swing for one to stand within your walls, and tell those men out there on your sidewalks that they are full of the God inspiration and may have their provisions straight from God by laying hold of the all-providing Spirit, and that by so doing they will find their sidewalks swept and garnished by miraculous winds, you have enough truth to make you bold.

The lily toils not, but its work is perfect. Jesus Christ toiled not, but his work rides majestically prosperous over the crumbled walls of ancient Rome, whose architects are forgotten. Had the Romans thrown over building temples and watched the wonderful one Spirit that Jesus was watching, their work too would be alive today.

There is one source of knowledge. There is but one knowledge. That is God. We need not be afraid our debts will not be paid if we are laying hold upon the owner of the stars. We need not fear that our children will go hungry if we are telling what we know is true of the here-present Jehovah.

It is not what we know of stones as stones that will give us support. It is what we know of the God inside and outside the stones that will feed us. While the world has been working with things as things, torturing matter for its knowledge, it has been in "Haran," the dry place. It has had angels, namely, great moments of inspiration, which have come down with sudden miracles of help in times of panting anxiety. It has put up noble statements from its soul center toward the heights. These also are angels.

Angels of ascending are proclamations of truth that work with the One Spirit. Angels of descending are the results of those proclamations. While we are in dry places, hungry, tired, anxious, we see our past few great thoughts going up to bring down help. But what if we had had only true thoughts every moment?

The Priceless Knowledge of God

Can I know anything worth knowing except God? While I am studying or working at anything else I shall wait and faint on the plains of effort, effort, effort. The primeval man pounded his nut against a stone till he wore his heart and hopes out, but still was struggling to get the meat. Then an angel turned his hand over and he pounded the stone on the nut and was fed. He who studies less than the One Spirit is pounding his nuts on stones.

How hard it has been for Jacob, the congregation of the church, to get his living by killing animals regardless of their shrieks, killing men on battle fields, employing little children, manufacturing merchandise! A fortune today, the poorhouse tomorrow, starvation in that garret, Crimean dainties in that palace — this is pounding nuts on stones. But lift up your heads, ye sons of men! God's presence bright is never absent. Truth on rounds of glory ascendeth now from the hearts of certain among us who, by attending unto God alone, find the promises of Jesus Christ really true. Take no thought saying, how shall we be provided for in this desert place, for your heavenly Father careth for you? *"Not by might nor by power, but by my spirit, saith the Lord."* (Zechariah 4:6)

Jacob need not have been in Haran the dry time. We need not have been in desolation. The church need not now be finding herself incompetent to help the shrieking throngs. But being in

63

Haran, lo! that which Jacob said, "The Lord gave me the kids," having also been said by us, now brings down its blessings. In such an hour as we think not to be helped, God shall swing the true things he once spoke of himself down to our protection and providing and strengthening.

"If thou hast spoken truth enough

To hold thy thoughts aloft always,

Thy light shall always shine,

Thy strength shall never fail,

Thou art not less than God himself."

Inter-Ocean Newspaper March 11,1894

LESSON XI

Temperance

Proverbs 20: 1-7

There are three interpretations to be made of the texts of this day's lesson, as there may always be made three interpretations of all texts of the scriptures of all peoples. Take this text to start out with: "Ye shall drink any deadly thing and it shall not harm you." First, literally: Ye shall be able to drink strychnine solutions without being poisoned, because your body shall become poison-proof through acceptance of my religion.

Second, ideally: Ye shall be able to take any false idea into your mind and not be decided thereby, because your mind shall become idea-proof through acceptance of my religion.

Third, spiritually: Ye shall take of that spirit here and everywhere present whose breath is the swallowing up of all substances, and yourself shall be all spirit, and that without effort or trial of any sort.

If mind appreciates that the Lord is present it is drinking a deadly thing. For "the earth is clean, dissolved before me, saith the Lord." While mind has ideas roaming around in it discussing or contemplating poisons, material, like arsenic or alcohol, mind is sure to find its ideas all dissolved if it turns its attention to the awfully deadly spirit of the Lord forever near it.

If you are still thinking how severe the intemperance of man is it is certain you have not for one instant looked at the Lord. One look would annihilate your ideas in the twinkling of an eye. It is an "earth" mind and has to be "dissolved."

If you are thinking of how severe and harmful false religions are to the mind and character then it is evident you have not yet looked toward the spirit of the Lord. One look thereto would dissolve all your ideas that false doctrines do any hurt. You are still an "earth" mind while your ideas roam around eating notions of good and evil. "Behold I destroy both the righteous and the wicked together," saith the Lord. "The righteousness of the righteous shall not save him and the wickedness of the wicked shall destroy him. No man can see my face and live."

Therefore the only deadly thing is God. Nothing can stay in its estate which drinks one sight of God. Yet the doctrine of Jesus makes it easy to drink all of the omnipresent spirit and be lost. *"He that thus loseth himself shall find himself." "He that attendeth unto me alone I alone am within him." "We will make our abode in him."*

Only One Lord

By thus contemplating Bible passages we fulfill the prophecies that "In that day there shall be one Lord and his name one." In chemistry several substances may unite and take up less room than either one of them alone. Many substances chemically united take up no room at all. All the religions uniting shall be swallowed up by the truth common in them all. All ideas shall be dissolved by one look. All the books now on earth, whose multitude no man can number, shall be swallowed up by one book.

"In that day one and his name one." Even reading in these paragraphs of this fact is drinking the deadly God; but remember the promise: "It shall not hurt you." Hearing once of the deadly principle your dissolving has begun. You cannot get away from its subtle operations, now proceeding through the race mind. It does not even need your ear or your eye. It needs some of your acquiescence: It is now making nothing of your bodies and making nothing of your minds; its dissolving presence is that irresistible poison to heaven and sea and land physical and metaphysical. The March 18 lesson is "Temperance." It is selected from Proverbs, 20:1.7. Notice that it is literal, ideal, and spiritual in every text thereof. The international committee divides it into heads as teaching concerning wine: that it has (1) "terrible power;" (2) it ruins the soul; (3) it is an enemy to prosperity and success; (4) its cure is understanding of God.

If understanding of God is the dissolving of "terrible things" then it is our business to spend all our time understanding God. Understanding of God is always made synonymous with looking toward God in our Bible, and indeed in all bibles. "Understanding is a well spring of Life." "Look unto me and ye be saved." "With all thy getting, get understanding." "I am understanding." "Turn to me and live."

What King Alcohol Does

Verse 2: "The fear of a king is as the roaring of a lion." The fear that a powerful king excites is as if a lion were roaring near ready to pounce on an unarmed victim. King Alcohol excites the fears of armies of people. They sometimes flinch in cowardly fashion when he enters their homes, sometimes they rise bravely and crusade against him.

But it is written that "the Lord he is King, and there is none beside him." Do you cure a disease by describing its greatness or by describing the Lord as the only greatness? Shall you cure men of drunkenness by describing its terribleness of Jehovah? Is not our God "terrible as an army with banners? Who shall see his face and live? Doth he not now proclaim, "Turn unto me?"

"Fear of the King is fear of the Lord. Fear means singleness of eyesight, both of mind and body." If thine eye be single thy whole body shall be full."

See only one king. No other king can abide in that house whose one inmate only recognizes one king only. "The Lord, he is king!" God is the only presence; that which is not God is the nowhere presence. Therefore "King Alcohol" is nowhere, nobody, and nothing but an idea which is melted by one turn of the eye toward the Lord who is king.

"Every fool will be meddling." Literally we know how exasperating "fools" are. They disappear when they turn to ideas or when ideas are turned upon them. Ideally stupid imaginations interfere with good judgment "change ideas," said Socrates. Spiritually there is no fool like the Lord. He sees nothing, hears nothing, yet turns and overturns nations, churches, homes, interfering or "meddling" with everything and everybody "till he whose right it is to reign shall come."

"Who is blind like my messenger, or deaf as the servant in whom my soul delighteth?"

"My messenger is not concerned whether his bed be hard or soft, whether his food be slow to serve him or prompt, whether his meat be hot or cold. My messenger is not concerned whether he be sick or well or dead or alive."

"Two things hide the eyes from sight of me, namely, covetousness and aversion. Wish for nothing, not even righteousness. Look at me; I am present at all times. Dislike nothing, not even intemperance in virtue whereby a man is made most disagreeable. I am present at all times. I dissolve both the temperate and the intemperate. He who sees me interfereth everywhere with all things and all people. He who sees me, seeth nothing else."

Stupefying Ideas

Verse 4: *"The sluggard will not plow, therefore in harvest shall have nothing."* Literally, we have seen how sluggards always depend upon others to do for them what we have an idea they should do for themselves. Ideally a sluggish idea, is a stupefying factor in any mind. One stupefying idea is that we are responsible for the happiness and unhappiness of ourselves and our comrades. The worm is a great believer in responsibility. Considering the worm and calling ourselves worms of the dust has bread a great inertia of mentality so that the well informed seem to be few, while the ignorant swarm. Considering the unresponsible lily of the field is sure to feed us, clothe us, shelter us. In the "harvest" that follows looking steadily at the lily there is no idea of lack, want, starvation. Spiritually, the Lord is the only sluggard there is. Being everywhere at the same instant he doth not have to hurry up. Being all there is in heaven above or earth beneath or waters under the earth there is nobody to ask to feed or clothe him. As he hath all things in himself it is always harvest time he needeth not look forward. Recognizing things as nothing but thoughts, recognizing thoughts as nothing, he himself being all and all else nothing, his "havings" are nothings, therefore it is the Lord who "hath nothing", or no-thing.

Verse 6: *"A faithful man who can find?"* Literally, Diogenes and his candle do not discover him. Ideally, what good and capable idea have you concentrated upon long enough for it to be master now of your business, your health, your judgment, so that there is nothing more for you to ask for or try for? Spiritually, it is no use for the good man to count on the Lord punishing the unrighteous or rewarding the wicked. The Lord is unaware of their existence, therefore cannot be faithful unto them. The Lord cannot be found. "Can a man by searching find out God?" No, for that which has to search after God is that which the presence of God dissolves. The spiritual interpretation of Scripture verses heralds the end of the world.

Inter-Ocean Newspaper, March 18, 1894

LESSON XII

Review and Easter

Mark 16:1-8

The science of the letter of scripture is now very clearly understood by civilized mankind. It is not disputed when a religionist of the literal order proclaims that certain courses of conduct result thus and so. "You must forego that sense claim," said a man's physician, "or you will lose your eyesight. *"Vale Lumen amjcum,"* (farewell light) sorrowfully replied the man. The sense appetite was master of him and not he of it.

On this plane we read in Telang's translation of the Bhagavad-Gita, p.50: "Objects of sense draw back from a person who is abstinent; not so the taste for those objects. But even the taste departs from him when he has seen the Supreme."

The teachers of mental science have been for several years insisting that if a man, with strong sense claims, will take a certain set of thoughts into his mind and keep them, running through his

waking, conscious ideas he will find his sense appetites falling away without struggling to be
abstinent therefrom.

They would tell us to think that "all is mind."

They would have us repeat, "There is no sensa-
tion in matter." They have a reason for this
"truth," as they call it, in the premise that "God is
the only mind of the universe and man." Of course,
then, there is no matter, for God is not matter. "I
call the world to battle on this issue," wrote an
ardent advocate of the Berkeleian philosophy,
"that matter is but appearance formulated by
states of consciousness."

Socrates taught that bad conduct is the result
of erroneous ideas. Change a man's ideas and his
conduct changes. "Ideas are the only real things,"
said Plato.

Words of Spirit and Life

On this plane most of the translations of scripture texts have been made by the mental scientists
who have called themselves Christian scientists
because they have discovered that Jesus Christ
was talking their principle when he said: *"The
flesh profiteth nothing: the words I speak unto you
are spirit and life." "If a man eat the bread (word)
that I will give him he shall never die."*

Then there is the purely God interpretation of
scripture texts. Last Sunday's lesson demanded
the full presentation of this interpretation. As the
literal school of thought, insisting on reform

schools, prisons, and pledges of abstinence, objected to the purely mental treatment of "badness," so the mental scientists rose in startled objection to the purely God interpretation of last Sunday's texts.

In science we must have one watchword, viz.: "On!" If I ever did one breath of my speech of mind or tongue say "God is omnipresent," I have then to say, "All is God." And on that plan I have to work the texts of all the Bibles of the world. So I make God the "deadly thing" of which Jesus spoke. Many verses of the sacred writ confirm this understanding. What is indeed, more deadly than that which, if you even "look upon" it, will kill you? And is not our God so deadly that "no man can look upon his face and live?"

"This is pernicious instruction," some say, "and ought to be stopped." No, for Jesus in the next words comforts me, saying, "I shall not hurt you." So I rise up boldly on his assurance and know that God is the one omnipotent energy who cannot be overthrown when proclaimed. I shall have mind slain, my body dissolved by looking toward the blazing splendor of "Thou Only," but thou shall be my life and my intelligence, and am I not glad thus to lose my life in order that I may find it?

Facing the Supreme

As Christians we here touch pages with the Brahmins, who teach: "Even appetites, depart from him who faces the Supreme." "God is Spirit." He who studies spirit loses materiality.

What did the Christian scientists mean, by saying, "All is spirit," if they were not expecting to show forth their spiritual substance utterly unclothed of flesh? What did the physicians mean by looking into metaphysics if they did not expect physics to disappear? "Let physics beware of metaphysics," said Newton.

It glorifies God and honors him forever if I leave the flesh or literal text of last Sunday's chapter and make it all God. As this day's lesson is "Review and Easter" I will repeat the wonderful tidings of death to matter and thoughts in the text, "The sluggard who does not plow shall have nothing in harvest."

He who is everywhere at the same instant does not have to move on, or observe times and seasons. He is subject not at all to springtime and winter. He is the "Great Sluggard" of omnipresence. He is God.

Having all things now he has his harvest all in now and forever. Things and thoughts being dissolved in his sight they are nothing. And hereby is our God the "Great Haver of Nothing." It is true that this upsets and cuts the thews of my literal and platonic renderings, but it is compelled by my saying. "God is the only life and only substance." Again I rest on the promise of Jesus: "Ye shall drink any deadly thing (doctrine)] and it shall not hurt you." And again I rest on the doctrine of death: "He that, would save his life must lose it."

Looking backward from that set of texts, I find Jacob at Bethel. Two years ago last November the scripture lesson chosen by the international committee compelled the discovery that when the gospel of Jesus Christ is truly read we find that, if there is "no sin, no sickness, no death," then there is no punishment for them. It was put under the head of "law and gospel."

Erasure of the Law

John said that the law "was the patience and faith of the saints." Jesus taught erasure of the law. John said the saints looked with gloating gladness to the law that "he that taketh the sword shall perish by the sword." Jesus told the thief that paradise is now here and never heard of stealing or punishment for sin. He put back the severed ear of the soldier to assure him that he was not necessarily a sufferer for his own false ideas.

Jacob saw his error erased. His physical hearing dissolved for a moment, his thoughts ceased their noisy murmurings. His spiritual ear heard the voice of the Supreme. He suspended both physical and metaphysical process. He unwittingly practiced the two "yogas" now so much talked about. He entered the region of being where both carnal body and carnal thinking are unknown. Whoever enters here leaves sin, sickness, death, law of cause, punishment for conduct behind.

Do not imagine that it is essential to bring this principle to your remembrance. You hear it referred to often by those who, after careful observation, see it plainly, but if you were not told it again after that lesson of two and one-half years ago you would one day and yourself announcing it as something you had discovered yourself. Once let a true interpretation of Jesus stir through the electric ethers of this age and every man shall say it is what he always believed.

Do you imagine that it is license to sin to say that sin is delusion? Then you belong to the literal plane. The practice of change of thought would expose to you a remarkable principle, viz. that negation is annihilation. If you have a bad temper, mentally proclaim, "I have nothing bad about me." Watch how indifferent you will soon become to provocations. You will indeed be more like unto the "Great Indifferent," whose silence here in our midst shows his unprovokableness.

If you imagine that misfortune and oncoming decrepitude belong to you as a physical being try denying them and see how they will fall away and fall away till by some mystic sense you recognize your immortal authority over sin, death, and the grave.

Need No Other Friend

If you have caught any beam if the face now looking into yours I tell you that you need no other friend. "Thou art my high counselor, my noble comrade, my rich and powerful champion!" The smile of the supreme on your face is enough.

The "Easter" department of this day's lesson has for its golden text: "Christ is risen." If Christ is risen then your hardships are rolled away already. On the flesh plane you may struggle on and compete with this age for your bread and butter. You may be a cart driver or non-employed boy. You may be a millionaire or an anxious father of seven little hungry babies. You will not have your clash with your stone at the door of the place where Christ is hidden any result but old and lagging head and hands and feet.

It is written that the two Marys went forth realizing what a hard worldly state of affairs hid them from the miracle-working God. If you attempt to solve your problem by metaphysics you will find your daily affairs much easier. Many a difficult task will roll itself aside. You may feel half like a shirk by such a process, but it is the way "angels" work. The "angels" *had already rolled away the stone for the two Marys.* (Mark 16:1-8); "Our thoughts our angels are."

But here in our midst is our miracle working God, who needeth not our efforts of mind or body. Christ is God. If I look upon this presence I must not say, "When the new dispensation arrives we shall be happy." Why should I speak of a time to come when there will be no poor and no rich, no black and no white? Are not these ideas dead forever when I see Christ the here and present miracle worker? Is not the idea of future gone if I now see God face to face?

Who is this that talks of time and progression, of the "steady gain of good principles?" It is he who has one eye on the flesh with its restraining thoughts and its practices of commerce, church, school, and government. Take thine eye off these things at their struggles. He is not in delusions. Turn this way, our Christ now risen works all the mighty miracles while we are still gazing, and only gazing.

The letter interpretation of scripture is passed away. The mental science style of rendering served its faithful purpose. The Christ of all the texts has its irresistible splendor swallowing them all in its risen statements. I preach the science of God and there is no world with whom to call battle on this issue, for I do not believe in any other world but the world of God.

Inter-Ocean Newspaper, March 25, 1894

Notes

Other Books by Emma Curtis Hopkins

- *Class Lessons of 1888 (WiseWoman Press)*
- *Bible Interpretations (WiseWoman Press)*
- *Esoteric Philosophy in Spiritual Science (WiseWoman Press)*
- *Genesis Series*
- *High Mysticism (WiseWoman Press)*
- *Self Treatments with Radiant I Am (WiseWoman Press)*
- *Gospel Series (WiseWoman Press)*
- *Judgment Series in Spiritual Science (WiseWoman Press)*
- *Drops of Gold (WiseWoman Press)*
- *Resume (WiseWoman Press)*
- *Scientific Christian Mental Practice (DeVorss)*

Books about Emma Curtis Hopkins and her teachings

- *Emma Curtis Hopkins, Forgotten Founder of New Thought –* Gail Harley
- *Unveiling Your Hidden Power: Emma Curtis Hopkins' Meta-physics for the 21st Century (also as a Workbook and as A Guide for Teachers) – Ruth L. Miller*
- *Power to Heal: Easy reading biography for all ages –Ruth Miller*

To find more of Emma's work, including some previously unpublished material, log on to:

www.highwatch.org

www.emmacurtishopkins.com

WISEWOMAN PRESS

1408 NE 65th St.
Vancouver, WA 98665
800.603.3005
www.wisewomanpress.com

Books Published by WiseWoman Press

By Emma Curtis Hopkins

- *Resume*
- *Gospel Series*
- *Class Lessons of 1888*
- *Self Treatments including Radiant I Am*
- *High Mysticism*
- *Esoteric Philosophy in Spiritual Science*
- *Drops of Gold Journal*
- *Judgment Series*
- *Bible Interpretations: Series I, thru XII*

By Ruth L. Miller

- *Unveiling Your Hidden Power: Emma Curtis Hopkins' Metaphysics for the 21st Century*
- *Coming into Freedom: Emily Cady's Lessons in Truth for the 21st Century*
- *150 Years of Healing: The Founders and Science of New Thought*
- *Power Beyond Magic: Ernest Holmes Biography*
- *Power to Heal: Emma Curtis Hopkins Biography*
- *The Power of Unity: Charles Fillmore Biography*
- *Power of Thought: Phineas P. Quimby Biography*
- *Gracie's Adventures with God*
- *Uncommon Prayer*
- *Spiritual Success*
- *Finding the Path*

Watch our website for release dates and order information! - www.wisewomanpress.com

List of
Bible Interpretation Series

with date from 1st to 14th Series.

This list is complete through the fourteenth Series. Emma produced at least thirty Series of Bible Interpretations.

She followed the Bible Passages provided by the International Committee of Clerics who produced the Bible Quotations for each year's use in churches all over the world.

Emma used these for her column of Bible Interpretations in both the Christian Science Magazine, at her Seminary and in the Chicago Inter-Ocean Newspaper.

First Series

85

Second Series

Third Series

January 3 - March 27, 1892

Fourth Series

April 3 - June 26, 1892

Lesson 1	Realm of Thought *Psalm 1:1-6*	April 3rd
Lesson 2	The Power of Faith *Psalm 2:1- 12*	April 10th
Lesson 3	Let the Spirit Work *Psalm 19:1-14*	April 17th
Lesson 4	Christ is Dominion *Psalm 23:1-6*	April 24th
Lesson 5	External or Mystic *Psalm 51:1-13*	May 1st
Lesson 6	Value of Early Beliefs *Psalm 72: 1-9*	May 8th
Lesson 7	Truth Makes Free *Psalm 84:1- 12*	May 15th
Lesson 8	False Ideas of God *Psalm 103:1-22*	May 22nd
Lesson 9	But Men Must Work *Daniel 1:8-21*	May 29th
Lesson 10	Artificial Helps *Daniel 2:36-49*	June 5th
Lesson 11	Dwelling in Perfect Life *Daniel 3:13-25*	June 12th
Lesson 12	Which Streak Shall Rule *Daniel 6:16-28*	June 19th
Lesson 13	See Things as They Are Review of 12 Lessons	June 26th

Fifth Series

Sixth Series

September 25 - December 18, 1892

Lesson 1	The Science of Christ *1 Corinthians 11:23-34*	September 25th
Lesson 2	On the Healing of Saul *Acts 9:1-31*	October 2nd
Lesson 3	The Power of the Mind Explained *Acts 9:32-43*	October 9th
Lesson 4	Faith in Good to Come *Acts 10:1-20*	October 16th
Lesson 5	Emerson's Great Task *Acts 10:30-48*	October 23rd
Lesson 6	The Teaching of Freedom *Acts 11:19-30*	October 30th
Lesson 7	Seek and Ye Shall Find *Acts 12:1-17*	November 6th
Lesson 8	The Ministry of the Holy Mother *Acts 13:1-13*	November 13th
Lesson 9	The Power of Lofty Ideas *Acts 13:26-43*	November 20th
Lesson 10	Sure Recipe for Old Age *Acts 13:44-52, 14:1-7*	November 27th
Lesson 11	The Healing Principle *Acts 14:8-22*	December 4th
Lesson 12	Washington's Vision *Acts 15:12-29*	December 11th
Lesson 13	Review of the Quarter	December 18th
Partial Lesson		
	Shepherds and the Star	December 25th

Seventh Series

Eighth Series

April 2 - June 25, 1893

Lesson 1   The Resurrection   April 2nd
Matthew 28:1-10
One Indestructible
Life In Eternal Abundance
The Resurrection
Shakes Nature Herself
Gospel to the Poor

Lesson 2   Universal Energy   April 9th
Book of Job, Part 1

Lesson 3   Strength From Confidence   April 16th
Book of Job, Part II

Lesson 4   The New Doctrine Brought Out   April 23rd
Book of Job, Part III

Lesson 5   The Golden Text   April 30th
Proverbs 1:20-23
Personification Of Wisdom
Wisdom Never Hurts
The "Two" Theory
All is Spirit

Lesson 6   The Law of Understanding   May 7th
Proverbs 3
Shadows of Ideas
The Sixth Proposition
What Wisdom Promises
Clutch On Material Things
The Tree of Life
Prolonging Illuminated Moments

Lesson 7   Self-Esteem   May 14th
Proverbs 12:1-15
Solomon on Self-Esteem
The Magnetism of Passing Events
Nothing Established by Wickedness
Strength of a Vitalized Mind
Concerning the "Perverse Heart"

Lesson 8	Physical vs. Spiritual Power	May 21st
	Proverbs 23:29-35	
	Law of Life to Elevate the Good and Banish the Bad	
	Lesson Against Intemperance	
	Good Must Increase	
	To Know Goodness Is Life	
	The Angel of God's Presence	
Lesson 9	Lesson missing	May 28th
	(See Review for concept)	
Lesson 10	Recognizing Our Spiritual Nature	June 4th
	Proverbs 31:10-31	
	Was Called Emanuel	
	The covenant of Peace	
	The Ways of the Divine	
	Union With the Divine	
	Miracles Will Be Wrought	
Lesson 11	Intuition	June 11th
	Ezekiel 8:2-3	
	Ezekiel 9:3-6, 11	
	Interpretation of the Prophet	
	Ezekiel's Vision	
	Dreams and Their Cause	
	Israel and Judah	
	Intuition the Head	
	Our Limited Perspective	
Lesson 12	The Book of Malachi	June 18th
	Malachi	
	The Power of Faith	
	The Exercise of thankfulness	
	Her Faith Self-Sufficient	
	Burned with the Fires of Truth	
	What is Reality	
	One Open Road	
Lesson 13	Review of the Quarter	June 25th
	Proverbs 31:10-31	

Ninth Series

July 2 - September 27, 1893

Lesson 1   Secret of all Power   July 2nd
Acts 16: 6-15   The Ancient Chinese Doctrine of Taoism
                  Manifesting of God Powers
                  Paul, Timothy, and Silas
                  Is Fulfilling as Prophecy
                  The Inner Prompting.
                  Good Taoist Never Depressed

Lesson 2   The Flame of Spiritual Verity   July 9th
Acts 16:18   Cause of Contention
                  Delusive Doctrines
                  Paul's History
                  Keynotes
                  Doctrine Not New

Lesson 3   Healing Energy Gifts   July 16th
Acts 18:19-21   How Paul Healed
                  To Work Miracles
                  Paul Worked in Fear
                  Shakespeare's Idea of Loss
                  Endurance the Sign of Power

Lesson 4   Be Still My Soul   July 23rd
Acts 17:16-24   Seeing Is Believing
                  Paul Stood Alone
                  Lessons for the Athenians
                  All Under His Power
                  Freedom of Spirit

Lesson 5   (Missing) Acts 18:1-11   July 30th
Lesson 6   Missing No Lesson *   August 6th
Lesson 7   The Comforter is the Holy Ghost   August 13th
Acts 20   Requisite for an Orator
                  What is a Myth
                  Two Important Points
                  Truth of the Gospel
                  Kingdom of the Spirit
                  Do Not Believe in Weakness

Tenth Series

Lesson 7	*II Corinthians 8:1-12*	November 12th
	Which Shall It Be?	
	The Spirit is Sufficient	
	Working of the Holy Ghost	
Lesson 8	*Ephesians 4:20-32*	November 19th
	A Source of Comfort	
	What Causes Difference of Vision	
	Nothing But Free Will	
Lesson 9	*Colossians 3:12-25*	November 26th
	Divine in the Beginning	
	Blessings of Contentment	
	Free and Untrammeled Energy	
Lesson 10	*James 1*	December 3rd
	The Highest Doctrine	
	A Mantle of Darkness	
	The Counsel of God	
	Blessed Beyond Speaking	
Lesson 11	*I Peter 1*	December 10th
	Message to the Elect	
	Not of the World's Good	
Lesson 12	*Revelation 1:9*	December 17th
	Self-Glorification	
	The All-Powerful Name	
	Message to the Seven Churches	
	The Voice of the Spirit	
Lesson 13	Golden Text	December 24th
	Responding Principle Lives	
	Principle Not Hidebound	
	They Were Not Free Minded	
Lesson 14	Review	December 31st
	It is Never Too Late	
	The Just Live by Faith	
	An Eternal Offer	
	Freedom of Christian Science	

Eleventh Series

January 1 – March 25, 1894

Lesson 1   *Genesis 1:26-31 & 2:1-3*   January 7th
The First Adam
Man: The Image of Language Paul and Elymas

Lesson 2   *Genesis 3:1-15*   January 14th
Adam's Sin and God's Grace
The Fable of the Garden
Looked-for Sympathy
The True Doctrine

Lesson 3   *Genesis 4:3-13*   January 21st
Types of the Race
God in the Murderer
God Nature Unalterable

Lesson 4   *Genesis 9:8-17*   January 28th
God's Covenant With Noah
Value of Instantaneous Action
The Lesson of the Rainbow

Lesson 5   I Corinthians 8:1-13   February 4th
Genesis 12:1-9
Beginning of the Hebrew Nation
No Use For Other Themes
Influence of Noble Themes
Danger In Looking Back

Lesson 6   *Genesis 17:1-9*   February 11th
God's Covenant With Abram
As Little Children
God and Mammon
Being Honest With Self

Lesson 7   *Genesis 18:22-23*   February 18th
God's Judgment of Sodom
No Right Nor Wrong In Truth
Misery Shall Cease

Lesson 8   *Genesis 22:1-13*   February 25th
Trial of Abraham's Faith
Light Comes With Preaching
You Can Be Happy NOW

Twelfth Series

Thirteenth Series

July 1 – September 30, 1894

Lesson 1   The Birth of Jesus   July 1st
Luke 2:1-16
No Room for Jesus
Man's Mystic Center
They glorify their Performances

Lesson 2   Presentation in the Temple   July 8th
Luke 2:25-38
A Light for Every Man
All Things Are Revealed
The Coming Power
Like the Noonday Sun

Lesson 3   Visit of the Wise Men   July 15th
Matthew 1:2-12
The Law Our Teacher
Take neither Scrip nor Purse
The Star in the East
The Influence of Truth

Lesson 4   Flight Into Egypt   July 22nd
Mathew 2:13-23
The Magic Word of Wage Earning
How Knowledge Affect the Times
The Awakening of the Common People

Lesson 5   The Youth of Jesus   July 29th
Luke2:40-52
Your Righteousness is as filthy Rags
Whatsoever Ye Search, that will Ye Find
The starting Point of All Men
Equal Division, the Lesson Taught by Jesus
The True Heart Never Falters

Lesson 6   The "All is God" Doctrine   August 5th
Luke 2:40-52
Three Designated Stages of Spiritual Science
Christ Alone Gives Freedom
The Great Leaders of Strikes

Lesson 7   Missing   August 12th

Lesson 8   First Disciples of Jesus   August 19th
John 1:36-49
The Meaning of Repentance

Fourteenth Series

October 7 – December 30, 1894

Lesson 1   Jesus At Nazareth   October 7th
Luke 4:16-30 Jesus Teaches Uprightness
          The Pompous Claim of a Teacher
          The Supreme One No Respecter of Persons
          The Great Awakening
          The Glory of God Will Come Back

Lesson 2   The Draught of Fishes   October 14th
Luke 5:1-11 The Protestant Within Every Man
          The Cry of Those Who Suffer
          Where the Living Christ is Found

Lesson 3   The Sabbath in Capernaum   October 21st
Mark 1:21-34 Why Martyrdom Has Been a Possibility
          The Truth Inculcated in Today's Lesson
          The Injustice of Vicarious Suffering
          The Promise of Good Held in the Future

Lesson 4   The Paralytic Healed   October 28th
Mark 2:1-12 System Of Religions and Philosophy
          The Principle Of Equalization
          The Little Rift In School Methods
          What Self-Knowledge Will Bring
          The Meaning Of The Story of Capernaum

Lesson 5   Reading of Sacred Books   November 4th
Mark 2:23-38 The Interior Qualities
Mark 2:1-4   The Indwelling God
          Weakness Of The Flesh
          The Unfound Spring

Lesson 6   Spiritual Executiveness   November 11th
Mark 3:6-19 The Teaching Of The Soul
          The Executive Powers Of The Mind
          Vanity Of Discrimination
          Truth Cannot Be Bought Off
          And Christ Was Still
          The Same Effects For Right And Wrong
          The Unrecognized Splendor Of The Soul

Notes

Notes

www.ingramcontent.com/pod-product-compliance
Lightning Source LLC
Chambersburg PA
CBHW060402090426
42734CB00011B/2236